EDINBURGH
OLD AND NEW

CATHERINE CRUFT

Published by EP Publishing Limited 1975

This edition first published 1975 by
EP Publishing Limited,
East Ardsley, Wakefield, Yorkshire,
England

ISBN 0 7158 1112 6

ep

Please address all enquiries to EP Publishing Limited
(address as above)

Printed and bound in Great Britain by
G Beard and Son Limited, Brighton, Sussex

Introduction

When I was asked to compile this selection of photographs for *Edinburgh Old and New*, I thought my task would be interesting and easy. With the wealth of early photographs available, the choice of material should have been simple.

Two problems made the undertaking harder.

Firstly, there is a paucity of early photographs of architecturally interesting parts of the city. It was the custom of the majority of early photographers to photograph the buildings of the city which were of historical interest to the tourist, rather than those of architectural quality. The result was that many photographs were taken of the Royal Mile, Holyroodhouse and the Castle.

The early commercial photographers were also attracted to Princes Street with its different styles of architecture and spacious gardens, particularly as the Scott Monument, the Royal Scottish Academy, the Calton Hill and the Castle provided ideal vantage points from which to view the street's development.

Thus much good architecture of the eighteenth and nineteenth centuries was ignored for the picturesque, the quaint and the panoramic postcard view.

Secondly, the trees and shrubs planted along the public walks and in the parks, as well as in the private gardens, have grown so as to obscure the exact view taken in some of the old photographs. These made a choice of photographs from the pathways along by the Water of Leith and from the Meadows and Princes Street Gardens, particularly difficult. These plantings conceal the views taken in the few early photographs of classical grandeur and Victorian domesticity.

My two photographers, Jim Mackie and Rod Ewart, with artistic skill and enthusiasm, strove to reproduce the identical views of the old photographs, but it was an impossible task to simulate the lenses used by earlier photographers.

I am greatly indebted also to the following who have generously given permission for photographs to be reproduced: Mr. Gerald Cobb, Mr. W. Nimmo, Robert Hurd and Partners, and the Librarian, the Royal Botanic Gardens, Edinburgh. My thanks, together with those of the photographers, also go to Miss C. S. Simpson, Heriot-Watt University, and the North British Hotel for permission to take photographs from their premises.

The negatives of the old photographs used in the book are Crown Copyright, Royal Commission on Ancient Monuments, Scotland, except for pages 51, 55, 59, 61 and 79 which are from negatives in the possession of Scottish Colorfoto Laboratories.

Catherine Cruft
Edinburgh, 1975

Contents

West Bow and Lawnmarket - c. 1875
On the corner stands the remaining fine example of a timber-fronted and jettied house. In 1835 the West Bow was partly demolished to make way for Victoria Street, built as an improved access road from the west. Further down the street are gabled houses of the early eighteenth century. In the distance St. Giles' Cathedral and the corner pilaster of the County Buildings are visible.

West Bow and Lawnmarket - 1975

In 1878 the timber-fronted house was replaced by tenements built as part of the City's plan for improvements. The next block was demolished in 1883. The gabled houses are still there, but the block on the corner has been replaced. St. Giles' Cathedral is still visible but the County Buildings were rebuilt in 1907.

Castlehill, Lawnmarket and West Bow - c. 1875

The timber-front of the West Bow is on the right. Somerville's Land on the left terminated a series of timber-fronted houses lining the Castlehill. It is a good example of better-class housing built for a burgess of Edinburgh and traditionally used by Mary of Guise after the destruction of Holyroodhouse by the Earl of Hertford in 1544. The neighbouring frontage, designed by Robert Mylne, His Majesty's Master Mason in 1690, was the first example in the Old Town of symmetrical planning. *Alexander Inglis*

3

Castlehill, Lawnmarket and West Bow - 1975
Somerville's Land was replaced in 1883 by an extension to the Free Church College. The Mylne block has been well restored and was adapted between 1967/70 for a University Student Residence. Next door is the eighteenth-century tenement of James Court. The neat wall-mounted street lighting at high level has been introduced for the whole length of the Royal Mile.

Mylne's Court, Lawnmarket - c. 1910
The open square behind the Lawnmarket facade is entered through a pend. Good well-planned housing has deteriorated to become overcrowded slum property. The Tolbooth Mission attempts to look after the needs of the children of the area, many of whom are barefoot. Window boxes brighten some window sills.

F. M. Chrystal

Mylne's Court, Lawnmarket - 1975
Restored 1967/70 after being condemned
in 1960. The block on the right has been
rebuilt with an ogee-cap added to the top
of the octagonal stair-tower. The rest has
been restored. The stairs are lit by
traditional type windows with fixed top
glass and movable wooden shutters.

Lawnmarket, North side - c. 1880

James Court, to the left, dates from 1725 and was well known to many of the famous, including David Hume, James Boswell and Dr. Johnson. The neighbouring tall narrow house, Gladstone's Land, was already built in 1631, when it was acquired by Thomas Gladstone, merchant. Decay has set in next door and partial demolition has already taken place. A temporary shop occupies the site. *George Washington Wilson*

Lawnmarket, North side - 1975
Although it is in bad condition on the north side, James Court is retained and Gladstone's Land (restored in 1935 by the National Trust for Scotland) can be seen complete with the arches of the old arcading which were discovered behind the shop front. They were formerly a common feature along urban street frontages. The remainder of the north side was rebuilt as part of the City Improvement scheme of 1893, under Professor Patrick Geddes; some original features were incorporated. The pend leads to Wardrop's Court, much of which was cleared away.

Lawnmarket, South side - c. 1910

A picturesque group of houses with small gables and pantiled roofs, dating from the seventeenth-century but partly rebuilt. In the centre an arched entrance leads to Brodie's Close. A later eighteenth-century block has been built on the corner of George IV Bridge, and beyond it can be seen the Old County Buildings.

F. M. Chrystal

Lawnmarket, South side - 1975
The right-hand block has been tidied up, but the corner block with its horizontal bands of masonry has been swept away together with Melbourne Place, and replaced by the new Midlothian County Buildings. The County Buildings of 1907 survive in the background. Surprisingly, the cobbles still remain, but the cobbled slope has been replaced by conventional steps.

Riddle's Court, Lawnmarket - c. 1910
Built in 1776 by Captain George Riddell,
it was renovated in 1893 as part of the
Lawnmarket Improvement Scheme.
F. M. Chrystal

Riddle's Court, Lawnmarket - 1975
Restored again in 1958/9 and converted
into flats and offices. New windows have
been inserted, but otherwise the
picturesque quality remains.

Greyfriars Churchyard - 1855/6

A view to the north-east from the historic churchyard. In the centre is the Magdalen Chapel, founded in 1541, with its steeple added in 1618. Behind can be seen the open crown of St. Giles' Cathedral. The building to the left of the Magdalen Chapel is the Highland Institute of 1836, one of the first buildings on the newly completed George IV Bridge, which is carried on arches over the Cowgate. In the foreground tenements and pantiled houses line Candlemaker Row.

Robert Keith

Greyfriars Churchyard - 1975
The Magdalen Chapel is obscured by trees and the crown of St. Giles' Cathedral is just visible above the buildings on George IV Bridge. The Central Public Library was built in 1890 and its roof can be discerned above the trees. The Highland Institute has become the Music and Art departments of the Library and stands to its left.

Grassmarket - 1855/6

The south side looking towards the Cowgate. In the distance can be seen the steeple of the Magdalen Chapel. On the left is the beginning of the West Bow. A group of seventeenth- and eighteenth-century tenements line the south side. They exhibit a mixture of height and forms. On the right is part of the block known as the Temple Lands, formerly the property of the Knights Templar and Knights of St. John. In front of the neighbouring tenement Captain Porteous was hanged in 1736. *Robert Keith*

Grassmarket - 1975
The corner of the West Bow has been restored and the neighbouring Greyfriars Hotel was rebuilt before 1879. A recent erection by the Bank of Scotland replaces some of the nineteenth-century rebuilding. The cobbled street remains, but trees and grass have been planted in the centre of the old market place.

Grassmarket and Edinburgh Castle - c. 1875
One of the most picturesque views of the castle. Clustered round the Castle Rock are the inns and warehouses of the Grassmarket where the principal horse and cattle markets were held. The new road, Johnston Terrace, cuts round the Castle Rock past the recently built military married quarters. *George Washington Wilson*

Grassmarket and Edinburgh Castle - 1975
The castle remains unaltered except for the addition of a new gateway from the esplanade. Most of the Grassmarket buildings have been rebuilt or refronted. In the distance can be seen the three spires of St. Mary's Episcopal Cathedral.

St. Giles' Cathedral - c. 1890
The historic core dates from the twelfth century and the ancient fabric was originally pressed close with the Luckenbooths. It was refaced and renovated in 1829 and again in 1879/83. On the left a line of Royal Mile tenements, dating from the sixteenth and seventeenth centuries, conceal the long closes behind. The low arcaded front of the City Chambers is visible as a break in the building line. A fine collection of lamp posts adorn Parliament Square.

Alexander Inglis

St. Giles' Cathedral - 1975
The cathedral remains the same and the Duke of Queensberry still stands sentinel by the clutter of parked cars in Parliament Square. The tenements each side of the entrance to the City Chambers were demolished prior to 1930, in order to build new extensions. The scaffolding round the Tron Kirk is just visible to the left of St. Giles, before the street drops steeply down to the Canongate and Holyroodhouse.

High Street and North Bridge - 1886

The timber-fronted house with the forestair was associated with the poet Allan Ramsay. Originally the house to the left had twin gables. Bunden's Temperance Hotel has wrought-iron balconies and floral window boxes.

21

High Street and North Bridge - 1975

Allan Ramsay's shop was cleared away c. 1898 for the grandiose scheme for the building on the southern approaches to the North Bridge. The part on the left was opened in 1906 for the Commercial Bank, now Royal Bank of Scotland, and Patrick Thomson's department store. The neighbouring tenements were decapitated in 1970, and the decorative wrought-iron balconies, seen in the earlier photographs, removed.

John Knox's House and Moubray House - c. 1900
The High Street narrows here with John Knox's house projecting. Condemned in 1849, it was saved for posterity by the intervention of Lord Cockburn. Adjacent to it is Moubray House. Both houses date from the sixteenth and seventeenth centuries. The association with John Knox is only by tradition. Beyond is the Moray Knox Church built in 1850. *J. Patrick*

John Knox's House and Moubray House - 1975
John Knox's House has again received a face lift and Moubray House is being restored. The Moray Knox Church has been demolished and replaced by the Church of Scotland Netherbow Centre. Further down the corner blocks of the Cousin and Lessels Scottish Baronial improvement housing of 1868 still just survive.

Chessel's Court, Canongate - c. 1910
The flats were built to look like a mansion house on the south side of a large court by Archibald Chessel c. 1748. In 1769 it became the Excise Office, and finally occupation was divided between tenants and the St. Saviour's Child Garden, a charitable kindergarten for local children.

F. M. Chrystal

Chessel's Court, Canongate - 1975
Restored and harled in 1963/4. The St.
Saviour's Child Garden still occupies the
ground floor. The remainder is divided into
private flats.

Canongate - c. 1890

On the right Moray House, built in 1628 for Mary, Dowager Countess of Home, is distinctive with its long first-floor balcony and twin gate piers with tall pyramid finials. Opposite stand seventeenth- and eighteenth-century tenements, including Bible Land and Shoemakers' Land. The clock on the Canongate Tolbooth, dated 1884, projects out over the street. *Alexander Inglis*

27

Canongate - 1975
Moray House remains carefully maintained; Bible Land and Shoemakers' Land and the other tenements were rebuilt in 1956 and set back from the original building line of the street. Some of the restoration preserved the original features and other parts were built in a traditional urban form with a ground floor arcading.

Canongate Tolbooth - c. 1890
Built 1592 as the civic centre of the
separate burgh of Canongate. The Council
Chamber is on the first floor reached by
the outside stair. It was restored in 1879.
The figures on the right are sitting on the
steps of the Market Cross. The forest of
washing poles was a frequent sight.

Canongate Tolbooth - 1975
The Tolbooth remains unaltered, but the seventeenth-century Bible Land was rebuilt 1956/8, and, adjacent, a new building was inserted exhibiting traditional street arcading. The cocoon visible up the Royal Mile, cradles the Tron Kirk in process of restoration. The Market Cross has been moved to the Canongate Churchyard.

Huntly House, Canongate - 1907

Dating from the sixteenth and seventeenth centuries, and named after George, 6th Earl and 1st Marquess of Huntly, it was originally built as three separate tenements and in 1647 was acquired by the Incorporation of Hammermen of the Canongate as an investment for accumulated funds. The three timbered and harled gables projecting over the lower floors dominate the front. The houses on the left exhibit the usual eighteenth-century gables, but one has a more sophisticated venetian window. The elegant ladies from the New Town still saunter down the Royal Mile for morning coffee or afternoon tea. *F. M. Chrystal*

Huntly House, Canongate - 1975

After a public outcry when it was threatened with destruction in 1924, Huntly House was restored by Sir Frank Mears as the City Museum. The small house to the left was finally restored in 1968/9 as part of the museum. Wilson's Court has gone and the next block has been rebuilt with a castellated wall-head.

Bakehouse Close, Canongate - c. 1910
Looking back down the close to the rear of Huntly House and through the pend to the Canongate. It was called Bakehouse Close after the Incorporation of Bakers who became owners of part of it.
F. M. Chrystal

Bakehouse Close, Canongate - 1975
Restored and tidied up as part of the
Huntly House restoration. Excrescences
have been removed. The harled portion to
the right is part of the restoration of 1968/
9. Its picturesque grouping is still retained
for posterity as a popular subject for
artists and photographers.

Whitehorse Close, Canongate - c. 1870
Stands at the foot of the Canongate near the Holyrood Sanctuary. Formerly it was one of the important inns of the city and dates from the seventeenth century. The north end of the close was an attractive subject for photographers with its twin wood-and-plaster gables and central fore-stair.

Whitehorse Close, Canongate - 1975
Partly rebuilt in 1889 as working-class housing and again restored in 1964/5 by the Corporation of Edinburgh and let to tenants. After the partial cost of restoration has been recovered by a cost-rent scheme, the flats are sold to sitting tenants.

Regent Terrace and Calton Hill - c. 1900
A photograph taken from Salisbury Crags showing the full range of Greek and Gothic revival building, from Calton Prison and the Governor's House to the beginning of Carlton Terrace. Holyroodhouse lies at the foot of the Royal Mile with Palace Yard in front. Breweries have been built around their local wells at the foot of the Canongate.

Regent Terrace and Calton Hill - 1975
The skyline remains unchanged except that St. Andrew's House replaced the Prison and Bridewell in 1936, and the top of the new St. James' Centre intrudes on the skyline. Regent Terrace is amazingly free from roof-line additions. Holyroodhouse has just been cleaned and the enclosing wall is the same. The breweries continue, but have replaced the old buildings with new.

Edinburgh - c. 1930
Looking towards the west from Salisbury Crags. Houses appear to have been built without an overall plan. The stepped terraced houses in Salisbury Street, 1819, are clearly visible in the centre but the rest is a mixture of improvement housing dating from the 1880's and 1930's.

39

Edinburgh - 1975
All the slum housing has been cleared away and probably the only regret is Salisbury Street. New model housing dating from the 1930's is seen in the centre. Recent flats are appearing up the valley, the rest is a vast car park. The new Students' refectory can be seen to the left opposite the McEwan Hall.

Bristo Street - c. 1910
A varied row of eighteenth-century tenements. The site of the Woolpack Inn, headquarters of the Carlisle Carriers, has been occupied since 1741. The most historic building is the harled tenement with the semi-circular upper windows. Connected with the beginnings of the Secession movement in Scotland, it was built in 1741 and the first floor was the manse of the Bristo Seceders; the arched pend led to the Meeting House. *F. M. Chrystal*

Bristo Street - 1975
The tenements have been razed to the ground in the last few years and the Students' refectory built as part of the University of Edinburgh new Student Centre.

George Square - 1954
The east side of the delightful square laid
out by James Brown about 1764. A
predominance of Roman-doric door pieces
adds distinction to these simple terraced
houses. The square was the first major
speculative residential lay-out built
outside the New Town.

George Square - 1975
After much controversy, the southern part of the east side has been demolished to make way for the erection of the William Robertson block, a part of the large building project by the University of Edinburgh on the site of three sides of the square. The Appleton Tower is visible above the remaining houses.

Summerhall - 1912
Part of the village of Summerhall dating from the late eighteenth-century. Shops have extended out into the gardens. Some splendid advertisements and second-hand furniture line the sides of the end house. *F. M. Chrystal*

Summerhall - 1975
The houses were demolished in 1912/13 for the building of the Royal Dick Veterinary College. The church was razed in order to extend the college. The latest addition can just be seen beyond the original building.

University of Edinburgh, South Bridge - c. 1900

Designed by Robert Adam, the foundation stone was laid in 1789, and the dome added by Sir Robert Rowand Anderson in 1886/7. The street was built in 1786/8 on a series of nineteen arches over the Cowgate. The grandiose plan for terraced shops and houses was eventually built to a simpler scale. *J. Patrick*

University of Edinburgh, South Bridge - 1975

The University building remains unaltered, and the South Bridge has changed little apart from the modern shop fronts. The South Bridge and Chambers Street corner has received a further addition. The Tron Kirk, surrounded with scaffolding, is visible in the background.

CALTON HILL EDINBURGH. FROM NORTH BRIDGE. 306.

Calton Hill - c. 1860
A view over the Waverley Station from the North Bridge. The railway has encroached on the remaining houses along North Back of Canongate. Everything on the hill was built between 1776 and 1830. The Prison, 1815, and the Bridewell, 1796, are on the right, and the Post Office, 1818, to the left. *Alexander Inglis*

49

Calton Hill - 1975

St. Andrew's House was built on the site of the Prison and Bridewell in 1936, so that only the Governor's House remains as a focal point. Waverley Station has been covered in, and a new Post Office built to the left; the old one being put to a different use, is concealed by a new extension to the rear.

Edinburgh from the Calton Hill - c. 1910
Eighteenth- and early nineteenth-century tenements climb up from the hollow of Greenside to the top of Moultray's Hill. The 195 ft. tower of the North British Hotel is a prominent landmark. *Alexander Inglis*

Edinburgh from the Calton Hill - 1975
All is cleared away to make way for the monumental bulk of the St. James' Centre, shopping precinct, hotel and government offices. The strange structure in the middle is a new bridge for pedestrians over Leith Street.

Edinburgh from the Calton Hill - c. 1890

A photograph looking to the west. Princes Street stretches for a mile in length. The Prison to the left was begun in 1815, and was originally intended for the south side of Princes Street. The Bridewell is being altered and the old North Bridge spans the valley between the Old and New Towns.

Edinburgh from the Calton Hill - 1975
St. Andrew's House has been built on the site of the Prison and the Bridewell, and its size conceals the new North Bridge, 1897. The North British Hotel, 1902, replaces the buildings along the north-west corner of the bridge.

General Register House and St. James' Square - c. 1910
The superb domes of General Register House, 1774 and 1869, and New Register House, 1856, viewed from the top of the tower of the North British Hotel. In the centre is St. James' Square, 1775, on Moultray's Hill. *A. Inglis & Co.*

55

General Register House and St. James' Centre - 1975
General Register House has been meticulously cleaned, and New Register House is to receive the same treatment.
Great changes have taken place, however, to the right. St. James' Square and the terrace along Leith Street have gone,
replaced by the St. James' Centre development. The west side of the square remains, much altered, as the Sasine
Office.

The Old Town - c. 1880

A view from the base of the Scott Monument looking over East Princes Street Gardens and Waverley Station. The rear of the City Chambers dominates the middle distance, and the crown of St. Giles' Cathedral is visible at the top right hand corner. Cockburn Street, 1860, was built as an access road to the station and divides the line of Market Street. The old North Bridge and the buildings on its southern approaches are on the left. *George Washington Wilson*

57

The Old Town - 1975
Trees obliterate the view to the left, where there is a new North Bridge and the Scotsman building of 1902. In the centre Cockburn Street survives dominated by a further addition to the City Chambers, 1930. The station has been roofed over.

Princes Street - c. 1895
A view taken from the Scott Monument looking towards the Calton Hill and Waterloo Place. The backs of the shops and tenements lining the North Bridge are seen on the right, and in front is the newly laid out garden on the roof of the Waverley Market. Shops and hotels line the north side of Princes Street. The Royal British Hotel and the Richmond Hotel stand on the corners of South St. Andrew Street. *Alexander Inglis*

59

Princes Street - 1975
The same view taken from ground level. (The Scott Monument was inaccessible because of repair work.) The North British Hotel replaced the shops on the North Bridge in 1902. Calton Hill and Waterloo Place remain essentially the same. Woolworths has taken over the corner of West Register Street, part of the Royal British Hotel has been rebuilt, and Forsyths, the first fully steel-framed building in Scotland, replaced the Richmond Hotel in 1906/7.

Princes Street - c. 1890
The old Waverley Hotel on the far side of South St. David Street. On this side stand Kennington and Jenner, and the Royal Hotel. On the right are the Scott Monument, 1844, and East Princes Street Gardens. The horse tram is on its way to Haymarket and Gorgie. *Alexander Inglis*

Princes Street - 1975
The Scott Monument is encased in scaffolding. The trees hide the old Waverley Hotel. Jenner's new building of 1895 replaced the original burnt in 1892, and is adjacent to the new Mount Royal Hotel. In 1965 British Home Stores replaced the North British Mercantile Building, just visible to the left in the early photograph.

Princes Street - c. 1900

A view to the west from the steps of the Royal Scottish Academy. On the right stand the New Club and Balmoral Hotel. Beyond Frederick Street are department stores and clubs. On the left can be seen the road up the Mound to the Old Town, and a corner of West Princes Street Gardens.

63

Princes Street - 1975
The New Club has gone, and part of the Balmoral Hotel demolished for premises for Littlewoods. The corners of Frederick Street remain almost unaltered except for the further addition of shop fronts. Further on, Boots has replaced its original building and Menzies has a new bookshop. Traffic signals clutter the roadway and the railings round the Royal Scottish Academy have never been replaced. All new buildings in Princes Street have to conform to the requirements of the statutory Princes Street panel, particularly in regard to providing an upper-level walk-way.

Princes Street - c. 1870
The Life Association of Scotland by Sir Charles Barry and David Rhind, 1858, and the New Club by William Burn, 1834. Two of the finest public buildings in Edinburgh.

Princes Street - 1975
Replaced in 1970 by a bank, shops and modern premises for the New Club.

View from the Castle - c. 1885

Princes Street with the complex of buildings behind. Charlotte Square is to the left, and the roofs of George Street run parallel with Princes Street. Moray Place is clearly visible. The country stretches away to the Firth of Forth with Fettes College, 1870, and its boarding houses in the centre. The Western General Hospital, 1867, is on the left.

J. Valentine

View from the Castle - 1975
All the buildings in Princes Street have been altered. Some higher roofs have appeared in George Street. Dr. Guthrie's monument, 1911, has been placed opposite the end of Castle Street. A string of playing fields, public parks and the Royal Botanic Gardens preserve a welcome belt of green.

Albert Memorial, Charlotte Square - c. 1910
The equestrian bronze statue of Prince Albert by Sir John Steele, 1870, stands in a formal layout of Victorian planting.
The surrounding square was designed by Robert Adam in 1791. *Professor Chrystal*

Albert Memorial, Charlotte Square - 1975
The Memorial is screened now by the growth of trees. The square and St. George's Parish Church remain unchanged externally. The church has been converted to a repository for the Scottish Record Office. The garden layout of 1871 vanished after the railings were removed in 1941. In 1946 new railings were erected enclosing the whole garden area. On sunny days in the summer the gates are unlocked and visitors allowed in.

Easter Coates House, Palmerston Place - c. 1890
Dated 1615 and built as a manor house for the Byres of Coates. Several sculptured stones from various locations in Edinburgh were built into the fabric during the restoration and adaptation for use as the Episcopal Cathedral Song School in 1879.

Old Coates House, Palmerston Place - 1975
Still used as a school, but now the St. Mary's Music School, with a further addition in 1904. To the left a new Song School has been built, and J. Oldrid Scott's Chapter House, 1891, appears to the right.

Dean Village - 1937
The remaining mills of the village viewed
from Thomas Telford's 108-ft.-high Dean
Bridge spanning the Water of Leith. In the
foreground is Jericho Mill, built in 1619,
one of the eleven water mills which
served the town of Edinburgh with meal.
On the left the coach house of Cabbie
James Stewart. Behind the mill chimney is
the West Mill of 1805. In the far distance
the twin open chimney towers of the
Dean Orphanage.

Dean Village - 1975
A disastrous fire in 1956 completely destroyed Jericho Mill. The three grindstones on the right mark the site of Lindsey's Mill. The chimney has gone, and the only remaining mill building, West Mill, has recently been converted into flats. The renovated coach house is now an architect's office.

Dean Village - c. 1900
Lindsey's Mill is on the right, West Mill is on the left. The photograph is taken from the eighteenth-century Old Dean Bridge. The Gothic landmark of the Holy Trinity Episcopal Church dominates the north end of the Dean Bridge. *F. M. Chrystal*

Dean Village - 1975
Lindsey's Mill disappeared in 1931, Holy Trinity Episcopal Church acquired a sanctuary in 1900, and in 1957 it was converted to an electricity sub-station. Seedling trees cover the banks of the Water of Leith.

Moray Place - c. 1855
The north-east corner of the 12-sided plan laid out and designed by James Gillespie Graham in 1822, on the Earl of Moray's feus. Mostly completed by 1827.

Moray Place - 1975
Many of the astragals have gone from the windows. No. 2 has an additional storey. It has also lost its balconies, and the foot of one of its windows has been raised. Legislation under the Town and Country Planning Acts controls future alterations of this kind in the New Town of Edinburgh.

The Royal Patent Gymnasium - c. 1875
The centre of a developing area near the Old Scotland Street Station where the gymnasium served as a place of recreation. The area is changing slowly. Old Canonmills House is visible in the trees to the right and in the centre is one of the four gas holders of the Edinburgh Gas Light Co., which supplied gas to the northern parts of the city; the backs of the houses in Brandon Street show up clearly. The mill-lade which originally ran into the Canonmills Loch can be seen along the rear of the gymnasium. *Alexander Inglis*

King George V's Playing Field - 1975
The gymnasium has gone and the site never fully developed. A row of garages hide the King George V's Playing Field.
Eyre Crescent and Eyre Place Church have been built in front of the backs of Brandon Street, on the site of Old
Canonmills House. The Scotland Street Station site remains undeveloped.

Royal Botanic Gardens - 1905
One of the oldest Botanic Gardens in the world, founded by two Edinburgh doctors in 1670 to provide cultivation of medicinal and other plants. The superb large palm house was built in 1858. The range of conservatories in front was constructed in 1898. The varying shapes make a pleasing effect.

Royal Botanic Gardens - 1975
Only the large palm house survives, peeping over the top of the new plant houses opened in 1967. The unique design depends for support on an intricate external structure of steel tubes and cable from which the glass is suspended. The design casts the minimum of shadows on the plants. The new creates as pleasing an architectural effect as the old.

The Foot of the Walk Leith.

Leith Walk - c. 1905
The area known as the Foot of the Walk, was originally the end of an unformed track across an open plain from Edinburgh to Leith. After the opening of the North Bridge in 1772 the wide carriageway was formed to finish here at the meeting of five principal streets.

Leith Walk - 1975
Architecturally the scene has hardly changed. The Central Station, on the right, survives, but is not in operation. The statue to Queen Victoria was raised in 1907. However, the new multi-storey Kirkgate House destroys the domestic scale. The large star on the roof can be illuminated and rotated into different shapes on festive occasions.

Kirkgate, Leith - c. 1910

A street scene throbbing with life. It is a centre for trade and shopping. On the right stands the New Gaiety Theatre, originally built as the Princess Theatre, and opened in 1889. A typical boot shop is on the opposite side of the street. Saturday night was the busy night when the head of the Kirkgate was the general meeting place.

Kirkgate, Leith - 1975
The thriving centre has been obliterated together with the medieval street pattern. Not one building survives at this point except the nineteenth-century corner tenement on the right.

Kirkgate, Leith - c. 1920

The continuation of the Kirkgate to Tolbooth Wynd and The Shore. The churchyard wall on the right encloses South Leith Parish Church. Opposite the church stands Trinity House, built in 1817, replacing the building of 1555, founded by the Incorporation of Shipmasters of the Trinity House of Leith, one of whose principal functions was and is the licensing of pilot boats. *J. R. Coltart*

Kirkgate, Leith - 1975
All the business and shop premises have gone, and have been replaced by housing as part of the Kirkgate development. Paving stones replace the cobbles, and Trinity House and the churchyard wall are the only visible survivors.

The Shore, Leith - c. 1910
Extends from the Signal Tower south to the foot of Tolbooth Wynd on the east side of the Water of Leith. The photograph spotlights a fine series of eighteenth-century houses, all with typical central gablets, some with crow-steps. The earliest block, the King's Wark, stands at the junction of Bernard Street, to the left. *F. M. Chrystal*

The Shore, Leith - 1975
Unfortunate changes with no thought to the original effective grouping. Only one pub remains, but the building above was replaced in 1912, and its neighbour has disappeared to be replaced with a recent flat-roofed structure. However, the King's Wark survives, and is in the process of restoration. The house next door has been lowered down to its good eighteenth-century doorway. The building of 1864 on the other side of Bernard Street remains.

The Citadel, Leith - c. 1910
Erected by General Monk in 1653 on the instructions of Oliver Cromwell, as a fortification, it was paid for partly by the Town Council of Edinburgh to protect their rights and privileges in Leith. By 1779, apart from the gate and portcullis, the Citadel had virtually disappeared. A later two-storey house has been built on the remains of the gate which acts as a vaulted pend to Johnston Street behind.

F. M. Chrystal

The Citadel, Leith - 1975
The house has been demolished and only the gateway survives because it is a scheduled monument. One of Leith's tower blocks, on the site of the Kirkgate, looms over the remains.

Newhaven Harbour - 1890

A fishing village from the sixteenth century, Newhaven was purchased by the City of Edinburgh from King James IV in 1510. Here the *Great Michael* was built in 1511 to be the largest ship afloat and the pride of the King's Scottish Navy. The present slip dates from 1812. The rear of the eighteenth-century houses in Main Street can be seen, and St. Andrew's Square and its closes are clearly visible. Fishing boats have been raised on to the beach at the rear of Main Street.

Newhaven Harbour - 1975
Land has been reclaimed from the sea to build warehouses still associated with the fishing industry. The buildings in St. Andrew's Square (now Fishmarket Square) and Westmost Close are in the process of restoration, and new housing is being built over the site of the raised beach. Newhaven is still a living community but a block of early twentieth-century flats has a disastrous effect on the skyline.

Granton Castle - c. 1905
A sixteenth- and seventeenth-century castle built in a commanding position on the shores of the Firth of Forth and occupied until 1794. Through the courtyard gateway could be seen a famous garden. Note the bicycles with the two foot bars for free-wheeling. *Professor Chrystal*

Granton Castle - 1975

The Castle was demolished c. 1920 and only the rectangular lean-to dovecote remains. This can be seen to the right of the roof of the seventeenth-century Caroline Park House. Just out of the photograph to the right are the Granton Gasworks, Edinburgh's major gas supply. The leafy lane has gone, and the western sea front planned in 1931 has been abandoned at this point.

Cramond Village - c. 1910

Part of the late eighteenth-century housing built for the workers in the iron mills on the River Almond. The cottage industry of nail making was also followed. Cramond Island can be seen in the background. *F. M. Chrystal*

Cramond Village - 1975
Now preserved as part of a restoration scheme for the whole village undertaken by Edinburgh Corporation. The house to the right, finally a popular café, has been demolished. The esplanade and the river continue as a popular haunt for picnickers and yachtsmen.